ROMANIAN POEMS

American Editions of Paul Celan's Writing

Poems of Paul Celan
Translated by Michael Hamburger
(New York: Persea Books, 1988)

Breathturn
Translated by Pierre Joris
(Los Angeles: Sun & Moon Press, 1995)

Threadsuns
Translated by Pierre Joris
(Los Angeles: Sun & Moon Press, 2000)

Selected Poems and Prose of Paul Celan
Translated by John Felstiner
(New York: W. W. Norton, 2000)

Glottal Stop: 101 Poems by Paul Celan
Translated by Nikolai Popav and Heather McHugh
(Hanover, New Hampshire: University Press of New England/Wesleyan
University Press, 2000)

Romanian Poems
Translated by Julian Semilian and Sanda Agalidi
(Los Angeles: Green Integer)

PAUL CELAN

ROMANIAN POEMS

Translated from the Romanian
and with an Introduction by
Julian Semilian and Sanda Agalidi

GREEN INTEGER
KØBENHAVN & LOS ANGELES
2003

GREEN INTEGER BOOKS
Edited by Per Bregne
København/Los Angeles

Distributed in the United States by Consortium Book
Sales and Distribution, 1045 Westgate Drive, Suite 90
Saint Paul, Minnesota 55114-1065
(323) 857-1115/http://www.greeninteger.com

First Edition 2003
©Suhrkamp Verlag Frankfurt am Main,
Published by in agreement with Suhrkamp Verlag
English language translation ©2003 by Julian Semilian and Sanda Agalidi
Introduction ©2003 by Julian Semilian and Sanda Agalidi
Back cover copy ©2003 by Green Integer

Design: Per Bregne
Typography: Guy Bennett
Cover: Photograph of Paul Celan

LIBRARY OF CONGRESS CATALOGING IN PUBLICATION DATA
Celan, Paul [1920–1970]
Romanian Poems
ISBN: 1-892295-41-5
p. cm — Green Integer 81
1. Title II. Series III. Translator: Julian Semilian and Sanda Agalidi

Green Integer books are published for Douglas Messerli
Printed in the United States of America on acid-free paper.

CONTENTS

Introduction   7

Regăsire   24
    Encounter   25
Cântec de dragoste   26
    Love song   27
Azi noapte   28
    Last night   29
Poem pentru umbra Marianei   30
    Poem for Mariana's shadow   31
Reveion   34
    Night of the New Year   35
[Orbiți de salturi uriașe]   36
    [Blinded by giant leaps]   37
Tristețe   40
    Melancholy   41
[Fără titlu, fragment dintr-un poem neterminat]   42
    [Without title. Fragment of an
      unfinished poem]   43
[Fără balustradă]   44
    [Without banister]   45

[A doua zi urmând să înceapă deportările]   48
  [The next day the deportations
    about to begin]   49
[Poate că într-o zi]   52
  [Perhaps one day]   53
[Din nou am suspendat marile umbrele albe]   56
  [Once again I suspended the great white
    parasols]   57
[S-ar putea crede]   60
  [It is conceivable one could believe]   61
[A sosit, în sfârșit, clipa]   68
  [Finally the instant is here]   69
[Partizan al absolutismului erotic]   70
  [Partisan of the erotical absolute]   71
[Erau nopți]   72
  [Those were nights]   73
Questions & Answers   76

Paul Celan's Romanian Texts

Paul Celan is known worldwide as a major, if not the greatest 20th century poet who wrote in German. Distinguished literary critics, historians and philosophers, from H. G. Gadamer to Jacques Derrida, have joined in the ever-growing bibliography of works on Celan. Biographers (perhaps the best known in English is John Felstiner), pay due attention to Celan's Eastern European origins, and overall, literary scholars have engaged quite comprehensively with his work. However most literary and hermeneutic discourse has focused on Celan's late poems, and little is known about his writings in Romanian. These include a group of poems and prose poems written during the time Celan spent in Bucharest, Romania's capital, between his departure from his native Bukovina in 1945 and his arrival in Vienna late in 1947. Despite, or rather because of their somewhat invisible status, these writings, translated here, seem to us precious and relevant, both textually and contextually.

Paul Celan was born in 1920 and grew up in Czernowitz, Bukovina's capital, shortly after the region was integrated in Greater Romania. During World War II his Jewish parents died in Transnistrian deportation camps, and at the war's end Celan himself was sent to a Romanian labor camp. In Bucharest between 1945-47, Celan finally crossed the border to Hungary and arrived in Vienna in 1947. In 1948 he moved to Paris where he married Giselle Lestrange, had a son, and spent the rest of his life as a poet, language teacher, and translator until his suicide in 1970.

Such biographical abbreviations can only hint at what Celan's poetry conveys to his readers. But one can easily recognize that the period in Bucharest is an obvious exception in Celan's life within the continuum of negativity which seems, after the war, to have fatefully and steadily lead the poet to grief and destruction, despite his literary success. For the years spent in Bucharest were the only non-melancholic years of his post-war life. It was in Bucharest that Celan became Celan, the anagram of Antschel, his original name. And it is in Bucharest where the texts included in this volume were written,

and his first published poem, "Todesfuge," appeared in Romanian translation as *Tangoul Morţii*, in *Contemporanul* in May 1947. In the poet's correspondence, and confirmed by Celan's closest friend, Petre Solomon, these years might be characterized not only as non-melancholic, but even touched with euphoria.

One might well wonder then why Celan didn't change his language from German to Romanian and stay on in Romania's capital instead of becoming an expatriate. After having fought—or having been compelled to fight—most of World War II on Hitler's side, the Romania of 1944 turned against its former ally. And as the war ended, the country, eager to redress its error, tasted hope, indeed experienced a cultural upsurge. However, once the last remnants of political opposition were liquidated and the Popular Republic of Romania was proclaimed in December 1947, the country was under the power of those who restrict thought and activity. This was indeed the time of Celan's departure from Bucharest; after a difficult and effortful border crossing to Hungary, he arrived in Vienna early in 1948. Sensing perhaps the totalitarian betrayal of anything the utopian left had ever

imagined, Celan left behind the Eastern parts of Europe, taking to the West his German language poetry and its unique message. Yet, with or without the Cold War, given Celan's larger mission, it seems unlikely that he would have stayed in Romania (1). What remains certain is that the Cold War added a sense of emergency, irreversibility and toxicity to his departure to the West, and it very likely influenced his decision not to stay in Austria or Germany, aggravating later his alienation in Paris. But also certain is that along with the Romanian texts, the years spent in Bucharest by Celan left unforgettable memories.

*

Celan wrote his first letter to Solomon soon after his arrival in Vienna. The letter narrates his passage through Hungary and arrival in Vienna, and ends with greetings sent to many friends to whom Celan did not have a chance to say goodbye at the time of his hurried and possibly secret departure. Many of those friends were great personalities in Romania's

culture, some still alive: artists, poets, intellectuals. Among them were the poet Nina Cassian (who later became the translator of Celan's poetry in both Romanian and English), Veronica Porumbacu, and Ovid Crohmălniceanu, the distinguished literary critic and historian who was the editor of *Contemporanul*. While the names Celan mentioned in his letter were those of his closest friends, the detailed picture provided by Solomon in his book suggests that the poet had a wider network of relations, which included the Romanian surrealists at its outer edge. In his letter Celan mentioned regretfully, the "too short season which was ours, *cette belle saison des calembours*, who knows when it will happen again, now that we don't play anymore *Question-Réponse...*." One might mention here that modern Romanian literary history matches overall, even if somewhat idiosyncratically, with Western literary history, with a strong avantgarde exisiting between the World Wars and a significant post-World War II surrealist chapter. Although surrealism is undoubtedly relevant to Celan's Romanian texts, however, it is also true that the *calembours* and Questions & Answers games –

versions of the well-known French *Cadavre Exquis*—
were not exclusively played within the surrealist group.
They were current within a far wider circle of writers
and artists who didn't identify themselves as
"surrealists," namely those with whom Celan kept
closest contacts. Solomon includes a sample of the
Questions & Answers game in his book, part of which
was originally handwritten by Celan.

"Cette belle saison des calembours" was Celan's way
of referring nostalgically to the skittishness and "come
what may" feelings released by the war just ended.
Indeed, an imaginary competing with and attempting
to outdo the harsh absurdity of the recent past,
charged the cultural climate, along with both hope
and fear for the future, with feverish intensity. The
surreality of life overlapped with, was actually
indistinguishable from, language and image-making
experimentation. "Conscious somnambulism" was the
way the Romanian postwar surrealists characterized
the spirit of the time before their manifestos and
literary productions were banned in the late 1940s.

Toward the end of his letter, Celan goes on to
convey his feelings of being different, an alien in

Vienna, a place which he seemed to detest and identified himself and his Romanian and Romanian-Jewish friends as levantines or Orientals, fondly remembering them and Balkan Burcharest. Celan's letter also includes sharp critical evaluations concerning the Viennese "literary milieu" and deep feelings of loss for what looked to him now as a too short "belle saison" for both him and his friends. "Where am I going? Where am I leaving you?" Celan asked, the questions compellingly and prophetically expressing his doubts about his own and his friend's future.

Celan's next letter to Solomon is dated ten years later, and, as with all of the letters after 1958 (with two exceptions) it was written in French. Celan felt that after ten years his Romanian had become rusty—or at least that is how he explained to his friend his unease with the language. Yet, when his earlier "Dragul meu Petrică" turns to "Mon cher Pierrot," to a Romanian speaker the shift feels abrupt, almost painful: from Petrică, which has a touch of voiced laughter in it, to Pierrot, and from the Slavic "dragul" to "cher" the distance is vast. Romanians use "mon

cher" jokingly to convey superficial intimacy—an irony which would not have escaped Celan, as well as the several other nuanced differences between the two languages. While Celan's attachment to his Bucharest memories, and his respect and love for his friends and colleagues left behind is reiterated in his French correspondence with Solomon, the expressive component, the playful conceits sparked by his use of Romanian in his first letter, proving his great intimacy with the language from the refined to the vernacular, are strikingingly absent. Instead, the leitmotif of loneliness reverberates like an echo. Between Celan's Bucharest interlude and his French letters to Solomon stand years of life in the West, the hurtful experience of its malignant cultural neuroses and the painful discoveries of postwar anti-Semitism. His decision not to write anymore in Romanian seems charged with secondary, unstated meanings.

*

Celan's correspondence which reveals his complicated relation to the Romanian language seems quite

relevant to his Romanian literary texts. Seen from a wider perspective, this relation assumes further significance.

Celan grew up and was educated in Northern Romania, with Romanian as the official language (as previously mentioned, Bukovina, part of Austro-Hungary before World War I was integrated into Greater Romania at the war's end, two years before Celan's birth). While Bukovina was an Austrian imperial province and Czernowitz, its capital was known as "little Vienna," German had been the main cultured language or "Kultursprache" for the Jewish community. After the integration, German continued to be spoken by Celan's parents at home and was taught to him by his mother. In the region's polyglot environment (besides German, Ukrainian, Romanian, Yiddish and Swabian criss-crossed the region), Romanian, accordingly, was not the major language, either as a practice or from cultural standpoint—despite its newly imposed "official" status. Also, in the economy of world literatures, Romanian language literature could not compete with German. It was in German, then, that Celan wrote his very first poems.

It was only his presence in Bucharest, where he was congenially surrounded by Romanian speaking Jewish-Romanians like himself, that resulted in the writing of his Romanian texts.

Aside from other considerations we suggest that Celan's shift to Romanian had interesting destabilizing effects that resulted from the frictions between his native German and the Romanian explorations. As the variables of Romanian upset the constants urged by German, unpredictable displacements enriched and reconfigured the ongoing linguistic positions that took place. It is similar to the case that Gilles Deleuze and Felix Guattari make concerning such destabilizations with reference to Kafka, and, in a broader, more historical vein, it reminds one of Václav Havel's statements in his essay "The Power of the Powerless." To Kafka's example, that of a Jewish Czech writing in German in Austro-Hungarian territories, Deleuze and Guattari add those of Beckett, Jean-Luc Godard and of another Jewish Romanian surrealist poet and artist Gherasim Luca, who, like Celan, whose friend he became in Paris, also was an expatriate: all bilingual or multilingual artists and writers, able to beneficially cross in and out of several modes of expression. They

all seem to fit the pattern of Celan's position in the linguistic discontinuum of his early years.

It is this destabilizing effect that manifests itself in Celan's writings in Romanian, where there is an abundance of refreshing modulations that seem to have been activated by the frictions between his native German and the Romanian—the latter, a Romance language structurally distinct from the Germanic. Celan also had become familiar with the surrealism in France, where he traveled in the late 1930s, so some French influences may have emerged as well in these Romanian texts. It would be interesting to speculate, moreover, how Celan's German was effected by the Romanian, and what might be the Franco-German aspect of Celan's poems at the time he lived in France, speaking French and writing in German. But these intriguing questions lie beyond our scope. What is clear is that these somewhat "secret" or private Romanian texts—texts he did not translate, publicize or intend to publish—reiterate the multilingual scope of his entire poetic creation, as well as inviting all the exciting questions stirred by today's postmodern, multicultural climate which busily revises and reverses the values previously attached to the marginal and

the "minor" (as opposed to the central, "major" and canonic), identifying history (literary or otherwise) as an inclusive rather than exclusive play of differences.

*

On the one hand, Celan's Romanian texts include his poems, most of which are titled and made up of stanzas which, although not rhymed, have a conspicuous rhythmic structure. On the other hand, the eight prose poems, which have a narrative flow and pace, are all untitled and consist sometimes of one single, half or full-page paragraph and at other times are broken into several paragraphs. The form of Celan's poetic prose written during the Bucharest years has been described as "ungewöhnlich" (unusual, exceptional, abnormal, odd, rare, strange) by critic Barbara Wiedemann—which indeed they are, even in Celan's own oeuvre. As Wiedemann points out, later prose pieces, such as "Conversation in the Mountains," a longer prose fiction written in the summer of 1959, are distinctly different from his Bucharest texts. Petre Solomon compares the early prose poems to "meteorites."

While one might argue that all of Celan's creations bear his mark, the prose poems are eccentric insofar as they approach an almost automatist stream of consciousness. The gambit for the translator (and perhaps this is the time to recognize Julian Semilian's primary role in the translations) is to parallel this eccentric linguistic momentum and at the same time confirm the Celanian voice.

Celan's Romanian texts, and this applies to both the poems and the prose works, revolve around a subjectivity striving to complete itself, but which unavoidably and fatefully lapses, is broken, cancelled by spatial and temporal collisions, stolen by language. While to a large extent these are the constants of Celan's poetic world (confirmed also by his Büchner Prize speech, "The Meridian," of 1960), the phonetic opennes of the Romanian language, its overall metaphoric rather than metonymic organiztion, its "innocence"—whether ontologically or historically understood—project the imcompleteness of the subject onto a horizon where accident and ellipsis destabilize the downturn, somehow maintaining an open commmunicative cycle. Although the narratives of progression from "early" to "late" may answer the

questions raised by this "openness," identifying the Bucharest texts as an early episode of Celan's development, we would posit that a major contribution to Celan's entire project was the adopted language itself. But, of course, while chasing the linguistic determinations which shaped the Romanian texts, their English translation unavoidably, de-canonizes the original, to borrow Paul de Man phrasing with reference to Walter Benjamin's "The Task of the Translator."

Although Celan's voice often seeped as if naturally into the English version, at times jugglery was required. In order to preserve in English the subtle Romanian idiom, and to maintin contact with the text's wider scope as well, betrayal and faithfulness to the original had to alternate. Thus certain untranslatable word-effects in the original had to be transformed in English; however, such transformations are subsequently compensated for by the choices which restore the overall tonality of the text.

In the stanza-poems, the interrupted and suspended dialogue tends to be spare, economically conceived. In the prose poems, on the other hand, the language becomes affluent, running into speedy dream-like

narratives, film-like montages of events. Endowed with preternatural lucidity, the highly mobile "I" of the prose poems is surrounded by multiple reflections and characters who resist, refuse, and obstruct his will. Constellations, exotic plants, archipelagos, monumental stairs, parasols, armies of trees, flaming wheels and acacias make up the scenery. While disaster seems to have already happened in the poems, in the prose poems it is about to happen. With the exception of the haunting hallucination in "The next day the deportations about to begin," there is no immediately recognizable historical or biographical reference in the prose poems, in them neologisms rub against the premodern and, with the one above mentioned exception, an overall feverish brightness and even an odd festive character reign. Yet, the very brightness and feverishness of these reports of confrontation convey the mood of feasts on the top of violence and seem to announce in their excess forthcoming sacrifice, omens of disaster which later reality confirmed.

—THE TRANSLATORS

Notes

1.   In his essay "Nu-l Dureau Numai Amintirile, Îl Durea Lumea," included in "Ochiul Meu Rămâne să Vegheze," published in *Caiet Cultural*, 3, 2000, pp. 33-45 (Bucharest) the Romanian poet Ion Caraion, who in 1947 edited and published in *Agora* three poems by Celan in German, makes interesting suggestions concerning Celan's decision to write in German rather than Romanian and his departure from Romania. Caraion thinks that his decision to publish Celan's three poems in German in the cosmopolitam journal (despite the fact that he had Romanian versions as well) influenced Celan's decision to discontinue his Romanian writing. Caraion also argues that Celan was influenced by Alfred Margul-Sperber, a poet whose opinion Celan very much respected. However, one must remember that German was, after all, Celan's native language.

ROMANIAN POEMS

Regăsire

Pe dunele verzi de calcar va ploua astănoapte,
Vinul păstrat pâna azi într-o gură de mort
Trezi-va ţinutul cu punţi, strămutat într-un clopot.
O limbă de om va suna într-un coif cutezanţa.

Şi-aşa vor veni într-un pas mai grăbit şi copacii,
s-aştepte o frunză cu glas, adusă-ntr-o urnă,
solia coastei de somn trimisă mareei de steaguri.
Scăldată în ochii-ţi să fie, să cred că murim împreună.

Părul tău scurs din oglinzi va aşterne văzduhul,
în care cu-o mână de ger voi aprinde o toamnă.
Din ape băute de orbi va sui pe o scară târzie
laurul meu scund, ca să-ţi muşte din frunte.

Encounter

Tonight it'll rain on the green dunes of limestone,
The wine preserved til today in the mouth of a dead man
will awaken the land of foot-bridges, displaced in a bell.
A human tongue will trumpet audacity in a helmet.

And thus the trees will arrive in a fury
to wait for the leaf that speaks, delivered in an urn,
the heralds of the coast of sleep sent off to the tide of
      banners.
Let it douse in your eyes, so I'll think that we'll die
      together.

Your hair dripping out of the mirrors will blanket the
      regions of air,
where, with a hand of frost, I'll set an autumn on fire.
From the waters imbibed by the blind my short laurel will
      scurry
up on a belated ladder, to take a bite from your forehead.

Cântec de dragoste

Când vor începe și pentru tine nopțile dimineața
Ochii noștri fosforescenți vor coborî din pereți, niște
    nuci sunătoare,
Te vei juca cu ele și se va revărsa un val prin fereastră,
Unicul nostru naufragiu, podea străvezie prin care vom
    privi camera goală de sub camera noastră;
O vei mobila cu nucile tale și-ți voi pune părul perdea la
    ferastră,
Va veni cineva și-n sfârșit va fi închiriată,
Ne vom întoarce sus să ne-necăm acasă.

Love song

When the nights begin for you at dawn
Our phosphorescent eyeballs will scurry down from the
      walls, chiming walnuts,
You'll juggle with them and a wave will crash in through
      the window,
Our single shipwreck, the translucent floor through which
      we'll peer at the vacant room below our own;
You'll furnish it with your walnuts and I'll suspend your
      tresses, curtains for the window,
Someone will come and it will, at last, be rented.
We'll return upstairs to drown alone at home.

Azi noapte

Din pomii sădiţi de amurg în odăile noastre incendiate
vom desprinde încet porumbeii de sticlă,
    frunzişul de-a pururi
foşnind, ne vor creşte pe umeri şi braţe, şi nu va fi vânt,
ci o baltă de umbre va fi, în care nu prinzi
    rădăcină,
un lac îngheţat, în care-şi dispută
    coroana de solzi înecaţii,
iar viaţa e barca la mal, părăsită de vâsle.
Un glas va veni dinspre flăcări spre noi să-şi păteze cu
    sânge argintul,
s-anunţe, întors în incendiu: Nu
    eu, ci ei singuri ştiu ora !
Şi-atunci vor porni din pustiu să-şi deşerte nisipul în
    preajma-ţi:
să fie şi munţi împrejur, să rămânem in Valea Tristeţii —
şi tu vei desprinde încet porumbeii de sticlă, arar, cîte
    unul,
iar când vor plesni în văzduh, vei vorbi în neştire cu
    mine.

Last night

From the trees planted at twilight in our arsoned rooms
we'll slowly unfasten the pigeons of glass, the foliage
      incessantly
rustling, they will sprout from our shoulders and arms,
      and there'll be no wind,
there will be but a mudhole of shadows, in which you
      will catch no root,
a frozen lake, where the drowned wrangle over their
      crown of scales,
while life is a boat on the shore, abandoned by oars.
A voice will march in from the flames towards us to stain
      its silver with blood,
to announce, from its place back in the fire: Not me, but
      they alone know the hour!
Then they'll set forth from the desert to spill their sand
      all about you:
let there be mountains around, we won't forsake the
      Valley of Gloom —
and you'll slowly unfasten the pigeons of glass,
      infrequently, one by one,
and when they burst in the air, you will speak deliriously
      to me.

Poem pentru umbra Marianei

Izma iubirii-a crescut ca un deget de înger.

Să crezi: din pământ mai răsare un braţ răsucit de tăceri,
un umăr ars de dogoarea luminilor stinse,
o faţă legată la ochi cu năframa neagră-a vederii,
o aripă mare de plumb şi alta de frunze,
un trup istovit în odihna scăldată de ape.

Să-l vezi cum pluteşte prin ierburi cu aripi întinse,
cum urcă pe-o scară de vâsc spre o casă de sticlă,
în care cu paşi foarte mari rătăceşte o plantă de mare.

Să crezi că e clipa acum să-mi vorbeşti printre lacrimi,
să mergem desculţi într-acolo, să-ţi spună ce ne e dat:

Poem for Mariana's shadow

Love's horsemint's grown like an angel's finger.

You must believe: out of the earth rises an arm twisted
     by silences,
a shoulder singed by the burning of turned out lights,
a face with the black mantilla of sight girdled about the
     eyes
a vast wing of lead, another of leaves,
a flesh wearied in the comforting sleep bathed by the
     waters.

Look! how it glides through the weeds with sprawled
     out wings,
how it mounts up mistletoe steps towards a building of
     glass
where, a sea plant aimlessly drifts with gigantic strides.

You must believe this is the instant to speak to me
     through the tears,
we must go there shoeless, to be told what awaits us:

doliul sorbit din pahar sau doliul sorbit dintr-o palmă—
iar planta nebună s-adoarmă auzindu-ţi răspunsul.

Ciocnindu-se-n beznă să sune ferestrele casei,
spunându-şi şi ele ce ştiu, dar fără să afle:
ne iubim sau nu ne iubim.

a death knell sipped from a cup or one sipped from a
        palm—
and the reckless plant will fall asleep with your answer
        in its ear.

Let the house windows clamor, clash
        in the dark,
let them confide all they know, to each other,
        still, they will never learn:
do we enrapture each other or not?

Reveion

În noaptea Anului Nou, anotimp fără ore,
ai trimis catafalcul cel tânăr să-ți cheme iubita;
au purces din oglinzi către ea și aprinsele lacrimi
în sfeșnicul nins de amar, răsărit dintr-o tâmplă.
Inelul stins în pahar s-a suit pe fereastră
s-o vadă venind prin zăpezi cu păr adormit;
s-au dus despletitele mâini s-o aștepte la poartă,
iar sus în odăi au venit să valseze poeții.
Dar ea a pășit peste prag să înfrunte o pleoapă,
să vadă la sânul ei treaz ațipind vietatea...

Un zar a căzut între lespezi, cu ochi de culoarea caisei,
iar turla cetății de lemn a plecat cu o umbră.

Night of the New Year

During the night of the New Year, season without hours,
you dispatched the young catafalque to petition your lover;
towards her the incendiary tears marched out of the
      mirrors
in the torch snowed over with sorrow, sprouting out of her
      head.
The ring extinguished in a cup perched up on the window
to spy her traipsing through snow with slumbering tresses;
the unbraided hands rushed to the gate to await her,
while above in the chambers the poets stepped to the
      waltz.
But she strolled through the threshold to fight back an
      eyelid,
to witness the quick of her wakening breast drift off to
      sleep.

A die tumbled between the slabs, with eyes of a nectarine
      hue,
and the wooden citadel's steeple left with a shadow.

[Orbiți de salturi uriașe] *

Orbiți de salturi uriașe, ne-am întâlnit, călători prin
      miragii, în singura sărutare-a renunțării.
Ora era cea de ieri, dar o arată un al treilea ac,
      incandescent,
pe care nu l-am văzut niciodată în grădinile timpului—
celelalte două zac îmbrățișate în sudul cadranului.

Când se vor despărți va fi prea târziu, vremea va fi alta,
acul străin va roti nebun până va aprinde orele toate cu
      un foc contagios
și le va topi într-o singură cifră
care-n același timp va fi oră, anotimp și cei douzeci și
      patru de pași ce-i voi face în clipa când voi muri
apoi va sări prin geamul plesnit în mijlocul odăii
invitându-mă să-l urmez ca să-i fiu tovarăș într-un nou
      orologiu care va măsura un timp mult mai mare.

[Blinded by giant leaps] *

Blinded by giant leaps, we met, wanderers through
      mirages, in the one kiss of renunciation.
The hour was yesterday's hour, but it was displayed by a
      third hand, incandescent,
a hand I never encountered in time's gardens —
the other two hands lie wrapped in each other on the
      south side of the dial.

When they part company it will be too late, the time
      will be another,
the alien hand will spin recklessly till it ignites all other
      hours with a contagious fire
and will melt them down to a single numeral
which simultaneously will be hour, season, and the
      twenty four steps I will take the instant I die

then it will leap through the cracked glass into the
      middle of the chamber
summoning me to follow it so I can be its comrade in a
      new clock which will measure a much greater time.

Eu, însă, prefer ca vremea să fie măsurată cu clepsidrele,
să fie un timp mai mărunt, cât umbra părului tău în
    nisip şi să-i pot desena conturul cu sânge, ştiind
    c-a trecut o noapte.
Eu, însă, prefer clepsidrele ca să le poţi sfărâma când îţi
    voi spune minciuna veşniciei.

Le prefer cum preferi şi tu părului meu cu sclipiri
    incerte şerpii,
prefer clepsidrele pentru că le pot sparge uşor cu toiagul
    amărăciunii
făcând să întârzie-n văzduh o aripă mare născută
    toamna şi care în timp ce mă culc lângă tine îşi
    schimbă culoarea.

* Poezia nu are titlu. Cel de faţă reprezintă începutul primulu
ivers. Intr-o copie manuscrisă, acest prim vers a fost şters de
autor cu creionul.

38

As for me, I prefer that time is measured with the
      hourglass,
let it be a time less tall, like your hair's shadow in the
      sand, and I will inscribe its outline with blood,
      knowing that a night has elapsed.

Yes, me, I prefer the hourglass so you can smash it when
      I tell you of eternity's lie

I prefer it just like you prefer to my hair with uncertain
      glimmers the serpents,
I prefer the hourglass because I can smash it easily with
      the walking-cane of distress
compelling a great wing born in autumn to linger
      behind in the breeze,
one which while I sleep next to you transmutes its hue.

* This poem has no title. The present title is the first line In
  the manuscript copy this line was penciled out by the author.

Tristeţe

Visele, volbura serii-auroră,
lac adormit într-un nufăr apus,
vii să le-ngheţi cu tăcerile, soră
neagră-a celui ce cunună ţi-a pus

cerul cu zimţi, de nea, peste tâmple,
nor înflorit, pe o geană să-l duci,
tu, rătăcită-n veşminte mai simple,
râzi: - oare mâine şi toamna din nuci ?

Iia n-o vrei, cea cu umbră cusută,
paing înstelat, peste noapte să-l pui...
Iar doarme aurul şi ceaţa se mută.
Cui îi dau roua? Lacrima — cui?

Melancholy

Dreams, eddies of evening's aurora,
slumbering lake in a sun-setting lily,
come, ebony sister, frost all in silence,
sister to him who crowned you with wreath

snowy pocked sky, blanket the brow,
on eyelash to ferry the flowering cloud,
laugh, rover in humblest of vestments:
tomorrow — the autumn of walnuts?

You won't suffer your shirt, sewn with the shadows,
spider of stars, to blanket the night...
The slumbering gold, the fog drifts afar.
Who longs for the dew? The tears — who?

[Fără titlu, fragment dintr-un poem neterminat]

Iarba ochilor tăi, iarbă amară.
Flutură vânt peste ea, pleoapă de ceară.

Apa ochilor tăi, apă iertată.

[Without title. Fragment of an unfinished poem]

The grass of your eyes, bitter grass.
Wind, billow above it, eyelid of tallow.

The water of your eyes, forgiven water.

[Fără balustradă] *

Fără balustradă, imensele scări pe care urcă și coboară steagul vaporos al întâlnirii cu tine însuți rămân singura coordonată sigură a mișcărilor care mă tentează încă. Fără balustradă, le accept totuși și chiar le prefer pentru rarele mele plimbări între Cancer și Capricorn, când, certat cu anotimpul, inund casa cu dantela neagră a plăcerii de a nu iubi pe nimeni. Tot atât de rar, dar sub un cer interior avertizat cu bagheta, cobor, o roată arzătoare, la marginea extremă a treptelor, până jos de tot, unde părul unei femei ucise de mine mă așteaptă pentru a mă strangula. Evit pericolul cu o abilitate care nu va trece asupra moștenitorilor mei. Apoi fac cale întoarsă și, ajuns la treapta de unde am pornit, repet performanța cu o viteză din ce în ce mai mare și până la batjocorirea spectaculoasă a coamei de pe treapta finală. Acum — și numai acum! — sunt vizibil pentru aceia care, dușmănindu-mă de mult,

term resenters of mine, await shivering the denouement. But, uneasy with episodes of this ilk, they think me the iron banister of the stairs, and unmindful of the hazard, they lumber to the utmost bottom, and throw open thoughtlessly, the portal through which the Defunct Illustrious will make her entrance.

---

* This prose poem and those that follow have no title. To help the reader, the first words of each text becomes the title.

[A doua zi urmând să înceapă deportările] *

A doua zi urmând să înceapă deportările, noaptea a venit Rafael, îmbrăcat într-o vastă deznădejde din mătase neagră, cu glugă, privirile arzătoare i se încrucișară pe fruntea mea, șiroaie de vin începură să-mi curgă pe obraz, se răspândiră pe jos, oamenii le sorbiră în somn. —Vino, îmi spuse Rafael, punându-mi peste umerii mei prea strălucitori o deznădejde asemănătoare cu aceea pe care o purta el. Mă aplecai înspre mama, o sărutai, incestuos, și ieșii din casă. Un roi imens de mari fluturi negri, veniți de la tropice, mă împiedica să înaintez. Rafael mă trase după el și coborârăm înspre linia ferată. Sub picioare simții șinele, auzii șuieratul unei locomotive, foarte aproape, inima mi se încleștă. Trenul trecu deasupra capetelor noastre.

Deschisei ochii. În fața mea, pe o întindere imensă, era un uriaș candelabru cu mii de brațe. —E aur?! îi

[The next day the deportations about to begin] *

The next day the deportations about to begin, at night Rafael showed up, mantled in a vast hopelessness of black silk, with hood, his burning gazes were crossing on my forehead, torrents of wine began streaming on my cheeks, they scattered on the floor, men sipped it in their sleep. — Come, said Rafael, placing over my too shiny shoulders a hopelessness not unlike the one he was wearing. I was leaning towards mother, I was kissing her, incestuously, and then, out of the house. A huge swarm of large black butterflies, in from the tropics, thwarted my advance. Rafael dragged me after him and we descended in the direction of the railway tracks. Under foot I felt the tracks, heard the whistle of a locomotive, very near, my heart tightened. The train rattled over our heads.

I opened my eyes. In front of me, across a huge expanse, stood a vast candelabra with thousands of

şoptii lui Rafael. —Aur. Te vei urca pe unul din braţe, ca, atunci când îl voi fi înălţat în văzduh, să-l poţi prinde de cer. Înainte de a se crăpa de ziuă, oamenii se vor putea salva, zburând într-acolo. Le voi arăta drumul, iar tu îi vei primi.

M-am urcat pe unul din braţe, Rafael trecu de la un braţ la altul, le atinse pe rând, candelabrul începu să se înalţe. O frunză mi se aşternu pe frunte, chiar în locul unde mă atinsese privirea prietenului, o frunză de arţar. Mă uit împrejur: nu acesta poate fi cerul. Trec ore şi n-am găsit nimic. Ştiu: jos s-au adunat oamenii, Rafael i-a atins cu degetele sale subţiri, s-au înălţat şi ei, şi eu tot nu m-am oprit.

Unde e cerul? Unde?

* Pe unul din textele dactilogratiate ale acestui poem in proză, apare titlul *Cerul,* şters însă cu creionul de către Paul Celan.

arms. — Is it gold?! I whispered to Rafael. — Gold. You'll crawl up one of the arms, so that, then, when I have lifted it up into the heavens, you'll hook it up to the sky. Before the break of dawn, people will be able to save themselves, flying there. I'll show them the way, and you'll welcome them.

I crawled up one of the arms, Rafael was shifting from one arm to the other, was touching them one after the other, the candelabra began to lift. A leaf fell on my forehead, on the very spot my friend had touched with his gaze, a maple leaf. I look all around: this cannot be the sky. Hours pass and I haven't found anything. I know: down there the people gathered, Rafael touched them with his thin fingers, and they lifted off, and me, I'm still rising.

Where is the sky? Where?

* On one of the typed copies of this text the title "The Sky" appears, penciled out by Paul Celan.

[Poate că într-o zi]

Poate că într-o zi, când reabilitarea solstiţiilor va fi devenit oficială, dictată de atrocitatea cu care oamenii se vor încăiera cu copacii marilor bulevarde albastre, poate că în acea zi vă veţi sinucide toţi patru, în acelaşi timp, tatuându-vă ora morţii în pielea frunzoasă a frunţilor voastre de dansatori spanioli, tatuându-vă această oră cu săgeţile timide încă, dar nu mai puţin veninoase ale adolescenţei unui adio.

Poate că voi fi în apropiere, poate că-mi veţi fi dat de veste despre marele eveniment, şi voi putea fi de faţă când ochii voştri, coborâţi în încăperile îndepărtate ale serei în care, în tot timpul vieţii, va-ţi exilat nesiliţi de nimeni, pentru a contempla eterna imobilitate a palmierilor boreali, când ochii voştri vor vorbi lumii despre nepieritoarea frumuseţe a tigrilor somnambuli... Poate că voi găsi curajul pentru a vă contrazice atunci, în clipa când, după atâtea aşteptări infructuoase, vom fi găsit un limbaj comun. Depinde de voi, dacă voi stârni, cu degetele răsfirate în evantai, boarea uşor sărată a requiemului pentru victimele primei repetiţii a sfârşitului. Şi tot de voi depinde dacă

[Perhaps one day]

Perhaps one day when the rehabilitation of solstices becomes official, required by the atrocity with which men will wrangle with the trees of the great boulevards of blue, perhaps on that day you four will finish yourselves, simultaneously etching the hour of your death on the leafy skin of your foreheads of Spanish dancers, etching this hour with the arrows yet timid, but no less venomous of the adolescence of a farewell.

Perhaps I'll be in your proximity, perhaps you'll bring me tidings of the great event, and I'll be there when your eyes, lowered in the distant chambers of the greenhouse, where, for the time yet alotted to you, you exiled yourselves voluntarily, so as to contemplate the eternal motionlessness of the boreal palm trees, when your eyes will voice to the world the unperishing delight of the sleepwalking tigers... Perhaps then I will find the audacity to contradict you, that instant when, after so much unfruitful waiting, we'll find a common tongue. It's up to you, if I incite, with fingers out like a fan, the faintly salted

îmi voi coborî batista în gurile voastre devastate de focul falselor profeţii, pentru ca apoi, ieşind în stradă, s-o flutur deasupra capetelor concrescute ale mulţimii, la ora când aceasta se adună lângă singura fântână a oraşului pentru a privi, pe rând, în ultima picătură de apă din fundul acesteia; s-o flutur mereu, tăcut şi cu gesturi care interzic orice alt mesaj.

De voi depinde. Înţelegeţi-mă.

windbreath of the requiem for the victims of the first rehearsal for the end. And likewise, it's up to you whether I lower my handkerchief into your mouths, devastated by the fires of a false prophecy, so that then, strolling out into the street, I'll brandish it above the concrescent heads of the multitude, at the hour when it assembles near the single fountain of the city, so as to gaze, one by one, into the ultimate drop of water at its bottom; yes, I'll brandish it incessantly, silent, and with gestures which forbid any other message.

It's up to you. Understand me.

[Din nou am suspendat marile umbrele albe]

Din nou am suspendat marile umbrele albe în văzduhul nopții. Știu, nu pe aici e drumul noului Columb, arhipelagul meu va rămâne nedescoperit. Nesfârșitele ramificații ale rădăcinilor aeriene de care am atârnat câte o mână se vor îmbrățișa în singurătate, neștiute de călătorii înaltului, mâinile se vor strânge tot mai convulsiv și niciodată nu-și vor lepăda mănușa melancoliei. Știu toate astea, precum știu, de asemeni, că nu mă pot încrede în mareele care, cu o spumă ca de jos, scaldă țărmurile dantelate ale insulelor acestora pe care le vreau ale somnului autoritar. Sub picioarele mele desculțe se aprinde nisipul. Mă ridic în vârful degetelor și mă înalț într-acolo. Nu mă pot aștepta la ospitalitate, știu și asta, dar unde să mă opresc, dacă nu acolo? Nu sunt primit. Un crainic necunoscut mie mă întâmpina în larg ca să mă anunțe că mi se interzice orice escală. Ofer mâinile mele însângerate de spinii plutitori ai cerului nocturn în schimbul unei clipe de repaos, în speranța că de acolo, de pe țărmul de mătase al primei despărțiri de mine, voi mai putea înălța un

[Once again I suspended the great white parasols]

Once again I suspended the great white parasols in the night's airy regions. I know, it is not through here the route of a new Columbus will stray, my archipelago will remain undiscovered. The endless ramifications of the aerial roots from which I suspended some hand will seek each other in solitude, the wanderer of heights will never know, the hands will grip one another in amplified convulsions, they will never peel off melancholy's glove. I know all this, just as I know that I can't put my trust into the tides, with foam as though from below, bathing the lace of the shores of these islands I yearn, islands of the imperious slumber. Under my shoeless feet the sand catches on fire. I lift up on the tips of my toes and hoist myself there. I don't expect hospitality, this I know, but where am I to pause if not there? I am not welcomed. A messenger I don't know greets me in the distance to declare that resting here is prohibited. I offer my fingers bloodied by the floating spines of the nocturnal sky in exchange for a moment's pause,

rând de pânze rotunde şi umflate şi că-mi voi putea continua călătoria înspre el. Ofer mâinile mele pentru a veghea ca echilibrul acestei flore postume să fie păstrat înafară de orice pericol. Din nou sunt refuzat. Nu-mi rămâne decât să-mi continui călătoria, dar mi-au sleit puterile şi închid ochii pentru a căuta un om cu o barcă.

in the hope that from the silken shore of the first parting from me, I might be able to raise a row of sails, circular and windfilled, and resume the journey there. I offer my fingers to oversee that the symmetry of this posthumous flora is kept away from any danger. Once again I am refused. All that's left me is to resume the journey, but my strength is nearly gone and I shut my eyes to look for a man with a boat.

[S-ar putea crede]

S-ar putea crede că tot ce s-a spus despre salcâmul-cruce ar ajunge să-ți interzică vacanța. Ai golit începuturile luminii din oglindă, te-ai desfătat cântând acrostihul neprihănitului călător întru miresme, mâhnit și clarvăzător ca floarea cepii, ai oftat cu prilejul basmalelor scuturate în grădini, ai chemat-o pe Mariana, ai chemat-o cu o culoare risipită odată cu cernelurile vieții, dar ai uitat că o încăpere nu e un copac, că frunzișul ei se mănâncă cu lingura amintirii și că ușile spre miazăzi sunt fără chei. Ai fi putut să pășești peste pragul lor înainte de revărsatul zorilor copleșite de avânturi îmbălsămate, să te reverși și tu odată cu lacurile din pereți, să sălți cu bulgării de zăpadă uitați în ochii tufelor antropofage, să mai spui odată—ultima dată— acel cuvânt care îți atârnă de icoana străvezie a gâtului tău neistovit: „rugină". Dar ruginie a fost însăși pustietatea în care te-ai aventurat cu sandala molipsită de poezia adolescenței tale de hârtie, ruginie a fost hârtia adolescentă peste care ai pășit până-n prag. Ai renunțat deci.

Ai hotărât să te sui în salcâm fără a depune efor-

[It is conceivable one could believe]

It is conceivable one could believe that all that's been disclosed about the acacia-cross is reason enough to rule out your furlough. You purged the origin of light from the mirror, you wallowed in lowing the acrostical of the chaste wanderer of the aromas, sullen and clear-sighted like the onion's flowering, you sighed on the occasion of the head scarf's spasm in the gardens, you summoned Marianna, you summoned her with a hue squandered along with the ink of living, but you were oblivious to the obvious evidence that a chamber is not a tree, that her foliage should be swallowed with Mnemosyne's spoon, and the portals to the South are lacking in lock-turning tools. You might have been able to skip over their threshold prior to dawn's deluge, dawn humbled by embalmed surges, to spill your own self along with the lakes in the walls, to leap with the snow drift left behind in the eyeballs of cannibal bushes, so that you can disclose one more time — the ultimate one — that word suspended by the translucent icon of your unrestricted throat: "rust." But rusty was the desert itself, the desert in which

turile precare ale cetitorului din stele. Stelele... De câte ori ai vrut să-ți reamintești eclipsa lor fulgurantă în mierea așternută pe masa cu otrăvuri... A fost un exercițiu din acelea care te-au făcut să părăsești orașul. L-ai părăsit ziua, în văzul tuturor, cu valiza îmbâcsită în creier, cu creionul resfirat deasupra amalgamului din ceară și primul pătrar al lunii.

Ce vesel era să împrăștii paharele cu murmur pe lespedea hexagonală a iubirii. Nimeni nu te vedea. Ai cutreierat singur străzile străjuite de umbréle enorme, parașutele piticilor din nou coborâți în pământ. Era un zvon în aer, un zvon de monede celibatare, venite să te vadă plecând. O clipă te-ai oprit să te uiți la ele: vestonul tău era descheiat și cum puteai să-ți satisfaci curiozitatea dantelată a pieptului tău, decât numai așa? Ți s-a vorbit de vizuini și mierle. Îndărătnic și

you ventured with your sandal contaminated by the poesy of your paper adolescence, rusty was the adolescent paper over which you skipped on your way to the threshold. Then you gave up.

You resolved to mount up to the top of the acacia blind to the precarious maneuvers of the star diviner. Stars...How often you craved to recall their fulgurant eclipse in the honey adorning the dining table studded with venoms... It was one daily drill among those that prompted you to forsake the metropolis. You did forsake it, in full daylight, under the scrutiny of the populace, suitcase soiled in brains, pencil out like a fan hovering above the alloy of tallow and the first quarter of the moon.

How delightful it was to squander the beakers of murmur over the hexagonal slabs of adoring. No one caught sight of you. You drifted alone across the avenues under the vigilant eye of the vast parasols, parachutes of gnomes sucked anew into the ground. There was a chiming in the air, a chiming of celibate coins, come to witness your departure. You rested a moment to peruse them: your mantle was undone and how could you allay the lace-work question mark in your chest, if not so? There were rumors of lairs and

pasionat de extremităţile alogene ale plimbărilor, ai crezut că sosise clipa pentru a le găsi, în ciuda moştenirilor paralizate. Te-ai înşelat şi aici.

N-ai văzut că paşii tăi înaintau spre plictiselile cu puf? Că vasta încăpere a posibilităţilor periclitate de ulii cu cercei nu mai corespundea steagului înfipt în balta cu oameni deghizaţi în bărci cu motor? N-ai înţeles că a fi călător îţi impunea perdeaua leproasă a corturilor însângerate? Ah, nu era nimeni în cort? Pe stema de la intrarea lui se instalase corbul rivalului? Corbul rivalului cu păr de ceai îngălbenit la lumina orei fără păsări? Ţi se cerea un act de curaj monosilab? O raită în priveliştea jefuită a imboldurilor vecine cu macul? Da, e greu să-ţi găseşti un loc acolo unde se păstrează un nisip răsfăţat între mâini de cărbune. E greu să duci cu tine visele orfane ale orbitelor îndoliate. E greu...

Dar spune, tu care ştiai să-ţi fluturi atrocităţile de lustru, strălucirile de obsedat al popasurilor arhipline de peştişorii dinţaţi ai veştilor fără frunze, tu mesager

blackbirds. Intransigent and enraptured of the allogeneic extremities of strolling, you surmised it was time to encounter them, despite the frozen inheritances. You were wrong again.

Couldn't you see your steps led you to the indifference of pillows? That the vast chamber of possibilities imperiled by falcons bedighted with earrings paralleled no longer the gonfalon impaled in the mudhole with men mimicking powerboats? Couldn't you fathom that to be a rover you were forced upon the leprosied curtain of the bloodstained tents? Ah, was there no one in the tent? Aloft the emblem, sentinel at the entry, wasn't that the rival's raven? The raven of the rival with the tresses of teas yellowed by the light of the birdless hour? Were you required to perpetrate a deed of monosyllabical audacity? A junket in the pillaged purview of the goading analogous to the belladonna? It's not easy to end up where they nurse a sand pampered with firebrand fingers. It's not easy to bear the orphaned dreamscapes of the orbits mantled with the death knell. It's not easy...

But tell me, you who were versed in fluttering your glazed delinquencies, the glimmerings of one haunted by the crossroads saturated with the jagged grunions

al abciselor înflorite cu sarea din lacrimi — răspunde:

Care s-a înecat întâi? Care a coborât treptele cu părul despletit și a înăsprit ondulațiile inegale ale posterității? Care a fugit din pieptul iubitei pe un cal furat la vecini? Care și-a ocolit mantaua, s-a... (*textul se întrerupe aici; pagina următoare lipsește*).

of leafless tidings, you, harbinger of abscissas brought to flower with lachrymal salt — answer me:

Who was the first to drown? Who scurried down ladders with mane undone and aggravated the misproportioned undulations of posterity? Who bolted from lover's breast on a steed abducted from the neighbors? Who steered clear of his cloak, has... (*the text ends here; the next page is missing*).

[A sosit, în sfârşit, clipa]

A sosit, în sfârşit, clipa ca în faţa oglinzilor care acoperă pereţii exteriori ai casei în care ţi-ai lăsat pe veci despletită iubita să arborezi, în vârful salcâmului înflorit înainte de vreme, steagul tău negru. Tăioasă, se aude fanfara regimentului de orbi, singurul care ţi-a rămas credincios, îţi pui masca, îţi prinzi dantela neagră de mânecile costumului tău de cenuşă, te urci în copac, faldurile steagului te cuprind, începe zborul. Nu, nimeni n-a ştiut să fâlfâie ca tine în jurul acestei case. S-a lăsat noaptea, pluteşti pe spate, oglinzile casei se apleacă mereu ca să-ţi culeagă umbra, stelele cad şi-ţi sfâşie masca, ochii ţi se scurg înspre inima ta în care şi-a aprins frunzele sicomorul, stelele coboară şi ele într-acolo, toate până la cea din urmă, o pasăre mai mică, moartea, gravitează în jurul tău, iar gura ta visătoare îţi rosteşte numele.

[Finally the instant is here]

Finally the instant is here, that instant when, facing the mirrors masking the facade of the dwelling where you abandoned, forever with outflaring hair, your lover, you hoist, atop the acacia precociously flowering, your black oriflamme. You listen to the razor-edged fanfare of the eyeless platoon, the last one to still worship you, you don the camouflage, you latch the black lace-work to the sleeves of your ashen costume, you scurry up the acacia, the folds of the oriflamme enfold you, now you are in flight. No, none knows how to billow like you about this dwelling. Night fell, you float on your back, the dwelling's mirrors squat to retrieve your shadow, the stars plummet down to lacerate your camouflage, the leak from your eyeballs speeds to your heart where the leaf of the sycamore caught on fire, the stars speed to your heart too, each to the very last, a diminishing bird, death, gravitates around you, while your dreaming tongue spills out your name.

[Partizan al absolutismului erotic] *

Partizan al absolutismului erotic, megaloman reticent chiar şi între scafandri, mesager, totodată, al halo-ului Paul Celan, nu evoc petrifiantele fizionomii ale naufragiului aerian decât la intervale de un deceniu (sau mai mult) şi nu patinez decât la o oră foarte târzie, pe un lac străjuit de uriaşa pădure a membrilor acefali ai Conspiraţiei Poetice Universale. E lesne de înţeles că pe-aici nu pătrunzi cu săgeţile focului vizibil. O imensă perdea de ametist disimulează, la liziera dinspre lume, existenţa acestei vegetaţii antropomorfe, dincolo de care încerc, selenic, un dans care să mă uimească. Nu am reuşit până acum şi, cu ochii mutaţi la tâmple, mă privesc din profil, aşteptând primăvara.

---

* Acest poem în proză e singurul care poartă, în manuscris, o dată precisă: 11.3.47.

[Partisan of the erotical absolute] *

Partisan of the erotical absolute, reticent megalomaniac even among the frogmen, harbinger, simultaneously, of the halo Paul Celan, I choose not to summon the petrifying physiognomy of the aerial shipwreck except at intervals of one decade (or more) and will not attempt skating except at the most belated of hours, on a lake patrolled by the gargantuan forest of acephalous members of the Universal Poetic Conspiracy. It's easy to see that around here you can't pervade with the arrows of a visible fire. A vast curtain of amethyst dissimulates, at the outskirts of the forest facing the world, the existence of this anthropomorphic flora, beyond which, I, selenic, will undertake a dance to stun me. I have not yet triumphed and, with eyeballs side-shifted to the temples, I spy myself in profile, awaiting seedtime.

* This is the only poem in the manuscript that bears an exact date: 3/11/47.

[Erau nopți]

Erau nopți când mi se părea că ochii tăi, cărora le desenasem mari cearcăne portocalii, își aprind din nou cenușa. În acele nopți ploaia cădea mai rar. Deschideam geamurile și mă urcam, gol, pe pervazul ferestrei ca să privesc lumea. Copacii pădurii veneau înspre mine, câte unul, supuși, o armată învinsă venea să-și depună armele. Rămâneam nemișcat și cerul își cobora steagul sub care își trimisese oștile în luptă. Dintr-un ungher mă priveai și tu cum stăteam acolo, nespus de frumos în nuditatea mea însângerată: eram singura constelație pe care nu o stinsese ploaia, eram Marea Cruce a Sudului. Da, în acele nopți era greu să-ți deschizi vinele, când flăcările mă cuprindeau, cetatea urnelor era a mea, o umpleam cu sângele meu, după ce concediam oștirea dușmană, răsplătind-o cu orașe și porturi, iar pantera de argint sfâșia zorile care

[Those were nights]

Those were nights when it appeared to me that your eyes, which I fitted with large orange circles, would enkindle their cinders. Those nights the rain rarely fell. I opened the windows and stepped up naked on the window sill to gaze at the world. The trees of the forest advanced towards me, one by one, prostrate, a vanquished armada advancing to lay down their weapons. I sat motionless and the sky lowered the standard under which it had dispatched its armadas into battle. From a cranny you stared at me, how I stood there, unspeakably entrancing in my bloodstained gymnosophy: I was the single constellation the rain did not extinguish, I was the Great Southern Cross. Yes, those nights it was cumbersome to open up your veins, while the flames engulfed me, the fortress of urns was mine, I filled it with my blood, soon after I discharged the rival armada, rewarding it with cities and harbors, while the silvery panther lacerated the

mă pândeau. Eram Petronius şi din nou îmi vărsam
sângele între trandafiri. Pentru fiecare petală pătată
stingeai câte o torţă.

Ţii minte? Eram Petronius şi nu te iubeam.

twilight that stalked me. I was Petronius and spilled my blood again among the roses. For each petal I stained you extinguished a torch.

Do you recall? I was Petronius and you didn't entrance me.

A sample of Paul Celan's surrealist "Questions & Answers"

— What is the poet's loneliness?
A circus act not included in the program

— What is a tear?
A scale awaiting a weight

— What is drunkenness?
A white page among colored ones

— What is forgetting?
An unripe apple stabbed by a spear

— What is returning?
Nearly nothing, but it could be a
snowflake

— What is the last night before departure?
Departing from an exhibit of antique
porcelains

GREEN INTEGER
Pataphysics and Pedantry

Douglas Messerli, *Publisher*

Essays, Manifestos, Statements, Speeches, Maxims,
Epistles, Diaristic Notes, Narratives, Natural Histories,
Poems, Plays, Performances, Ramblings, Revelations
and all such ephemera as may appear necessary
to bring society into a slight tremolo of confusion
and fright at least.

*

Green Integer Books

1 Gertrude Stein *History, or Messages from History* $5.95
2 Robert Bresson *Notes on the Cinematographer* $8.95
3 Oscar Wilde *The Critic As Artist* $9.95
4 Henri Michaux *Tent Posts* $10.95
5 Edgar Allan Poe *Eureka: A Prose Poem* $10.95
6 Jean Renoir *An Interview* $9.95
7 Marcel Cohen *Mirrors* $12.95
8 Christopher Spranger *The Effort to Fall* $8.95
9 Arno Schmidt *Radio Dialogs I* $12.95
10 Hans Christian Andersen *Travels* $12.95
11 Christopher Middleton *In the Mirror of the Eighth King* $9.95
12 James Joyce *On Ibsen* $8.95
13 Knut Hamsun *A Wanderer Plays on Muted Strings*
$10.95

14 Henri Bergson *Laughter: An Essay on the Meaning of the Comic* $11.95

15 Michel Leiris *Operratics* $12.95

16 Sergei Paradjanov *Seven Visions* $12.95

17 Hervé Guibert *Ghost Image* $10.95

18 Louis-Ferdinand Céline *Ballets without Music, without Dancers, without Anything* $10.95

19 Gellu Naum *My Tired Father* $8.95

20 Vicente Huidobro *Manifest Manifestos* $12.95

21 Gérard de Nerval *Aurélia* $11.95

22 Knut Hamsun *On Overgrown Paths* $12.95

23 Martha Ronk *Displeasures of the Table* $9.95

24 Mark Twain *What Is Man?* $10.95

25 Antonio Porta *Metropolis* $10.95

26 Sappho *Poems* $10.95

27 Alexei Kruchenykh *Suicide Circus: Selected Poems* $12.95

28 José Donoso *Hell Has No Limits* $10.95

29 Gertrude Stein *To Do: Alphabets and Birthdays* $9.95

30 Joshua Haigh [Douglas Messerli] *Letters from Hanusse* $12.95

31 Federico García Lorca *Suites* $12.95

32 Tereza Albues *Pedra Canga* $12.95

33 Rae Armantrout *The Pretext* $9.95

34 Nick Piombino *Theoretical Objects* $10.95

35 Yang Lian *Yi* $14.95

36 Olivier Cadiot *Art Poetic'* $12.95

37 Andrée Chedid *Fugitive Suns: Selected Poems* $11.95

38 Hsi Muren *Across the Darkness of the River* $9.95

39 Lyn Hejinian *My Life* $10.95

40 Hsu Hui-cheh *Book of Reincarnation* $9.95

41 Henry David Thoreau *Civil Disobediance* $6.95

42 Gertrude Stein *Mexico: A Play* $5.95

43 Lee Breuer *La Divina Caricatura: A Fiction* $14.95

44 Régis Bonvicino *Sky Eclipse: Selected Poems* $9.95

45 Raymond Federman *The Twofold Vibration* $11.95

46 Tom La Farge *Zuntig* $13.95

47 *The Song of Songs: Shir Hashirim* $9.95

48 Rodrigo Toscano *The Disparities* $9.95

49 Else Lasker-Schüler *Selected Poems* 11.95

50 Gertrude Stein *Tender Buttons* $10.95

51 Armand Gatti *Two Plays: The 7 Possibilities for Train 713 Departing from Auschwitz* and *Public Songs Before Two Electric Chairs* $14.95

52 César Vallejo *Aphorisms* $9.95

53 Ascher/Straus *ABC Street* $10.95

54 Djuna Barnes *The Antiphon* $12.95

55 Tiziano Rossi *People on the Run* $12.95

56 Michael Disend *Stomping the Goyim*

57 Hagiwara Sakutarō *Howling at the Moon: Poems and Prose* $11.95

58 Rainer Maria Rilke *Duino Elegies*

59 OyamO *The Resurrection of Lady Lester* $8.95

60 Charles Dickens *A Christmas Carol* $8.95

61 Mac Wellman *Crowtet I: Murder of Crow* and *The Hyacinth Macaw* $11.95

62 Mac Wellman *Crowtet II: The Lesser Magoo* and *Second Hand Smoke*

63 Pedro Pietri *The Masses Are Asses* $8.95

64 Luis Buñuel *The Exterminating Angel*

65 Paul Snoek *Hercules, Richelieu, Nostradamus* $10.95

66 Eleanor Antin *The Man without a World: A Screenplay* $10.95

67 Dennis Phillips *Sand*

68 María Irene Fornes *Abingdon Square* $9.95

69 André Breton *Arcanum 17*

70 Julio Matas, Carlos Felipe and Virgilio Piñera *Three Masterpieces of Cuban Drama* $12.95

71 Kelly Stuart *Demonology*

72 Ole Sarvig *The Sea Below My Window*

73 Vítězslav Nezval *Antilyrik and Other Poems* $10.95

74 Sam Eisenstein *Rectification of Eros* $10.95

75 Arno Schmidt *Radio Dialogs 2*

76 Murat Nemat-Nejat *The Peripheral Space of Photography*

77 Jean Frémon *Island of the Dead*

78 Stephen Ratcliffe *SOUND/(system)*

79 Dominic Cheung *Drifting* $9.95

80 Gilbert Sorrentino *Gold Fools* $14.95

81 Paul Celan *Romanian Poems*

82 Elana Greenfield *At the Damascus Gate: Short Hallucinations*

83 Anthony Powell *Venusberg*

84 Andreas Embirikos *Amour, Amour*

85 Herman Melville *The Piazza Tales*

86 Adonis *If Only the Sea Could Sleep*

87 Ingeborg Bachmann *Letters to Felician*

88 Paul Verlaine *The Cursed Poets*

89 Francis Carco *Streetcorners*

90 Knut Hamsun *The Last Joy*

91 Sheila Murphy *Letters to Unfinished J*

92 Toby Olson *Utah*

93 Louis-Ferdinand Céline *The Church*

102 André Breton *Arcanum 17*

Green Integer EL-E-PHANT Books (6 x 9 format)

EL-1 *The PIP Anthology of World Poetry of the 20th Century,*
Volume 1 $15.95

EL-2 *The PIP Anthology of World Poetry of the 20th Century,*
Volume 2 $15.95

EL-51 Larry Eigner *readiness / enough / depends / on* $12.95

EL-52 Martin Nakell *Two Fields That Fiace and Mirror Each
Other* $16.95

EL-53 Arno Schmidt *The School for Atheists:
A Novella=Comedy in 6 Acts* $16.95

EL-54 Sigurd Hoel *Meeting at the Milestone* $15.95

EL-55 Leslie Scalapino *Defoe* $15.95